PAIN, ANGER & TEARS IN ONE BLACK COVER BOOK

Pain, Anger & Tears

IN ONE BLACK COVER BOOK

(WITH A GLIMPSE OF SUNRISE)

Prisi R

Charleston, SC
www.PalmettoPublishing.com

Pain, Anger & Tears in One Black Cover Book

Copyright © 2023 by Prisi R

All rights reserved

No portion of this book may be reproduced, stored in a retrieval system, or transmitted in any form by any means–electronic, mechanical, photocopy, recording, or other–except for brief quotations in printed reviews, without prior permission of the author.

First Edition

Paperback ISBN: 979-8-8229-1650-0

Dedication

For my siblings all of them who held my hand through all my lowest points.

For my mom who had it harder than me and still had my back.

For my daughter Zoe who saves me every day and is the reason for my strength.

For my friends you know who you are. You saved me with every laugh, every meme and every touch.

For me.

Contents

My Heart in Pieces   1

My Old Man   69

Notes to Self   79

MY HEART IN PIECES

How miserable did I have to be to accept that shitty love you gave me.

How did I end up here?

And tonight I go to bed with a broken soul and a shattered heart.

I hope somehow I can fall asleep.

Maybe if I just stop thinking and close my

eyes I might also stop hurting.

Tomorrow in daylight I will smile and try again.

Life is sad for the most part.

Only sometimes you get happy.

Only sometimes you genuinely laugh.

Only sometimes you smile without forcing it.

Let's make that sometimes happen more often.

Anniversary

Today was supposed to be a day of celebration of our anniversary, to be exact but instead we fight, and we are separating.

You said some really ugly, hurtful things and I just took them and kept mine to my own.

One single tear dropped from my eye; that is the only one you will get from me.

I've been hurt in a very bad way, and
it meant nothing to you.

I gave you everything I was!!!

Now I don't know who I am.

I should just be happy I can breathe for a little bit!

The day I ran away for heaven I passed through hell.

I don't know for how long I will hurt.

Because it hurts, it really hurts.

Empty

I look at my finger; it has no ring.

I reach out with my thumb to touch it *(I use to play with it)* and is not there anymore.

My hand looks empty; my heart feels empty.

I miss it.

Strangers

We married without knowing each other.

Of course it didn't work out!

We were trying to be husband and wife to a complete stranger.

Drinking won't help

Partying won't make it go away.

Dancing may fade it a little.

Laughing only brings me back to crying.

So, I'll bury myself in books and movies once again.

Why is it that the right decision is always the hardest?

The most painful?

Someone?

Anyone?

I have it very clear that I will not be able to forget you.

So, the question is will I ever learn to live without you?

When you left, you took both my heart and soul;

 you should've taken my mind, too, because
now I only have all the memories of you.

Is there any version of my life where he is not in it?

Because I would love that very much.

Unfortunately, my alcohol tolerance went up since...

He is never going to change!

That is who he really is.

I need to cry.

I feel the tears inside of me; they want to come out.

I need to cry.

But I can't, something holds me back.

I needed to cry for so long now,

But I know that if I start crying, I won't be able
to stop and I don't have time for that.

I need to cry about so many things.

I share nothing. I silence myself too
much. I keep too much for myself.

But I also feel the more I hold my tears,
the more they dry inside of me.

*I need to cry and now I can't; maybe if I drag
those tears out of my soul it will be of some good.
I might shine a little, like a crystalline piece.*

Stop now?

My mind never stops.

It never lets me rest; it won't give me a break.

I'm tired, I'm exhausted, can someone

please tell my mind to stop now?

Her?

She is dying!

How?

I'm killing her!

Why?

She keeps getting hurt and disappointed.

So don't come back looking for her; she is almost all gone.

How is it possible to love and hate the same person with the same strength?

(She was surprised to hear her voice cracking with emotion.)

We don't always get what we deserve.

So, we accept what is given to us and try to live with it,

Just as it is.

Happy endings are stories that have not ended yet.

My laugh

is another way

of just not crying.

They lie when they say that time heals everything...

It's been time and I haven't healed.

I have to start all over again.

I have to learn to be alone, to be by myself with myself again.

I have to again invest time energy and heart in someone.

But honestly, I don't even know if I want to ever again.

Too

I guess it wasn't in the cards for me.

To have a happy ending.

Maybe, just maybe, in another life I get to be with the love of my life, I get to have everything I ever dreamed of.

But I think that ship has sailed probably in another life too.

I guess I fooled myself thinking that you were going to change, that you meant everything you said and promised me.

I guess the only one who wanted was me.

I gave my all to you because I love like that.

You only ended up helping me to forget and let you go.

He doesn't love me; it is obvious that he doesn't love me.

Because if he really did love me, even at some point

of his life, he wouldn't do what he does to me.

Right?

One word to describe today?

Pain.

I always get myself in this situation

Why do I keep getting myself hurt??

Fuck him.

And fuck him too!!!

I'm done. I'm so done.

And now I must relearn to be alone without feeling lonely.

I had already done that, then you came along and didn't stay.

I feel so out of place.

Like, like I am living someone else's life.

This is not me.

This is not me.

Where have I gone?

I am taking so long to come back.

Someone else is taking over my place.

I don't want it to be her.

I don't want to be in here no more; it's dark.

It's very dark in here.

I don't like how this feels.

I'm vanishing.

I'm locking my heart and I'm throwing the key into the ocean. I hope a whale or a shark eats it so nobody ever ever finds it again.

I can't...

It's going to take me more years to forget you than the years we were together.

It's going to take me ten new memories to replace one with you.

Everyone thinks I got this.

When I don't even know what this is.

Everyone thinks I got this.

I really wish we could've worked out.

It was you I wanted for my forever.

I was happy with my life.

And now I hate you for taking it away from me.

It's hard to accept what the mind knows but the heart can't comprehend, so all we do is let those tears fall from our face to our chest, hoping that one will get to the heart and fill it up somehow.

You took with you everything I ever loved...

You said I was your angel!!!

But I didn't realize that meant you were my devil.

It hurts so bad that the only thing left to do is laugh.

I lied when I said I was only going to shed one tear for this.

I have cried like never before.

I have screamed until my lungs can't no more.

I have laid in bed thoughtlessly staring into nothing.

And still I can't have the heart to do what you did to me.

Maybe it's because I have no heart left.

I used to wonder what it meant. "Window pain."

Now I don't wonder anymore.

I know what it means and what it feels like.

Yes, my pain does have a name and a last name.

No, I'm not ashamed of saying so, I'm only human.

I don't know how many color dyes my hair can take...

How do I cut someone from my life?

When I still love them.

I keep telling myself that he is not good for me.

But I don't find a way to let go; it seems the more I need to, the tighter I grab on.

My hands are bleeding.

My heart is hurting.

My eyes are burning.

I can taste my salty tears.

My veins are about to pop.

I need to let go.

Silent pain is the worst kind of pain...and this pain I discovered being with you.

You told me to go cry anywhere that was not in front of you and so I did.

You pushed me away over and over again, and still I stayed in till I broke the silence.

You broke me.

You ripped my heart from my chest, held
it in your hand, and played with it.

When you were done playing with my heart you put it
on the floor, stepped on it, and smiled while doing so.

I tried; I really did try.

But I had to stop trying when I realized it was making no difference...It was only me trying.

You didn't want me. You didn't want me.

Why didn't you want me?

Was something wrong with me? Or you?

These dumb questions keep replaying
in my head over and over again.

I can't understand; I just don't understand.

Do you even know why?

Now I don't want you and I do know why.

Now you want me?

I was yours to have.

Yours to enjoy and love and you didn't.

Now that I'm not yours, now you want me...

My response: GO FUCK YOURSELF!!!

With this, I say my last goodbye to you.

I have said goodbye crying.

I have said goodbye with kisses.

I have said goodbye with sex.

I have said goodbye with a hug.

I have said goodbye with a wave.

I have said goodbye over a call and text.

I have said goodbye screaming.

I have said goodbye whispering.

Today I say my last goodbye.

I have gotten so used to the taste of my own tears that I begin to miss it when I don't cry.

You are so selfish that you know you can come and go and come into my life again and make me a mess.

Please leave; leave for GOOD.

Go make a mess somewhere else.

I am afraid no one will ever love me for me.

That maybe I missed my chance.

That maybe you were it and we messed
it up for not knowing how to love.

I feel that with every time I laugh, I hurt a little less.

Why?

Why?

WHY?

WHYYY???

why?

I wonder how many more days of just sleeping three or four hours I can take before my body gives up.

Maybe I should just stay inside and feel the pain,

Feel how it consumes my soul.

Because of you, I'm scared of being too happy.

I'm scared of anything feeling beautiful.

I'm scared of falling for someone.

I'm scared of feeling vulnerable with anybody.

At what moment did we become strangers to each other while still being together...?

I ask him.

God!! Are you there?

Can you hear me?

Are you still with me?

Can I still be saved?

I'm numb.

I don't feel the tips of my fingers.

I think I'm drowning.

I think I'm gone.

Please please please...

I never thought I would be one of those sad people walking numb all the time.

I'm at the store or anywhere with my headphones on and not giving a shit about what goes around.

Yes, you did this to me...

I knew I deserved better and still stayed more than I had to.

I loved you with my heart, body, and mind,
and that wasn't enough for you.

I shared with you everything that hurt me.

I told you my weaknesses, my traumas,
and what I was scared of.

I also told you my fears and what I hated the most.

I gave you an open door to my heart
and everything that defined me.

YOU BETRAYED ME WITH EVERYTHING I SAID
ABOVE...YOU HURT ME IN THE WORST WAY.

I have just one question: Did you plan
it Or was it just an impulse?

I didn't know that the heart can
actually hurt—physically hurt.

I always thought it was just a figure of speech, but
I was wrong—so wrong—and I wish I wasn't.

Because the way you hurt me is how I
discovered this horrible truth.

The heart can actually hurt, and it
leaves an ache inside my body.

(But it does heal.)

MY OLD MAN

You were supposed to love me the most.

To show me what love really looks like...

And the only thing you did was to let me down and hurt me more than anyone.

You did not love us. You did not love me.
A parent does not do what you did; I know that now.
A parent does not pull your hair, does not call you useless
or idiot. A parent does not charge you for everything.

You say you don't remember that we struggled
with money...but we did; we didn't always have
enough for clothes, but you always had a nice suit
and your dressy shoes were well polished.

You say we didn't struggle with food? Yes, we did, and
mom always gave up her food, and if you take a good
look at every picture from the past, you can clearly tell.

I hate the flashbacks of your yelling and name-calling.
I hate the most realizing that we meant nothing to you.

A parent does not need to be told to
treat their kids nice, to show love.

*I remember when you made us kill that puppy...I
still hear his crying until he stopped.*

Narcissist: one word to describe you.

Where did you go? And why didn't you come back? And I'm not saying physically, because you have always been here.

You changed and not for good.

You lost yourself and didn't care.

Why did you leave?

You don't know the first thing about unconditional love.

You should've set her free a long time ago.

Not once did you ask us how we felt as we were
growing up. You never showed interest in what we
were going through or even asked "Are you okay?"

And when you wanted to, it was too late;
we were all grown up and we had already
learned to live this life without your help.

When it came to feelings or emotions, yours
were the only ones that mattered.

You.

You and you.

Why didn't no one stopped you from being mean to us? From being a bully?

Why didn't no one defended us?

Why didn't no one stand in front of you?

You hurt us!!

You hurt me!!

We have always been scared of you.

We are still scared of you.

Yes even till this day, even us the
grown ass adults that we are.

We tip toe around you; we are always ready
for any sudden movement or reaction.

We are still scared.

NOTES TO SELF

Never Forget Again

I had forgotten what was like to be me.

I had forgotten what was to smile and laugh without worries.

I had forgotten what was like to be free.

I had forgotten that I was pretty,

That I was fun.

I had forgotten that I was my own person
with my own heart, mind, and soul.

But, somehow, I remembered, and now
I never want to forget again.

Today I was happy.

Today I laughed.

Today I was myself.

Today I had no worries.

Today I was fun

Today needs to be repeated.

I don't know why I love myself, but I know that I do.

You got this, bitch!

She told the girl in the mirror...

You will see:

You will be happy again, just you.

I will look good.

I will feel good.

I will be confident again.

I will feel beautiful and sexy in my own skin.

I will love myself again.

I will.

We are allowed to break down a little,

Cry a little,

Shake up a little,

Stop for a little.

But when all those littles are over...

Get up, dry those tears, smile, adjust that crown, and take one step in front of the other.

Yes, I'm at the bottom right now...
but not for long; I will rise.

I believe in the love that heals, that helps you grow, that protects that saves.

And

I'm willing to wait for it.

I'm willing to do what it takes to have that love.

Today, I make this promise to myself:

I will have everything I ever dreamed of: the house, the car, the career, my business, and my books published.

It may take longer than I had planned; I will have to work harder for everything.

But I will make it.

12/01/22

I'm going to become the best version of myself for myself.

Stronger, brighter, confident, wiser,
so sure of who and how I am.

They will all regret having the chance of
treasuring me and not doing so...so badly that
it will give them chills to their bones.

I didn't know how good it felt to smile in between all my tears until I did it.

I felt relief.

I felt free.

I feel new.

I will not harden my heart because you broke me.

I will not darken my world because you decided to leave it.

I will not turn in to you.

Love yourself so much, so hard, so bad, that it doesn't matter or change anything if someone else does.

HURT...let it hurt all the way.

Let it hurt all that it needs to hurt.

And then let it go for good.

Thank him; thank him for forcing you to open your eyes.

Thank him for making you choose yourself

by him not choosing you.

Inhale all the good.

Exhale all the bad.

Breathe.

Breathe.

You got this; maybe not today, but one day.

You did it once all by yourself.

You will do it again.

But this time, better—this time you have experience.

I can forget him.

The answer to my question...is yes I can live without him and even better.

I'm glad he took my old heart, because I'm loving this new one I'm creating.

This is not the end,

This was only a chapter in your life story.

This is so not the end.

About the Author:

Priscilla Sarai is 31 and from San Antonio, Texas. She now lives in Del Rio, Texas with her daughter, Zoe. She has a cat named Peeta who has been with her for 13 years. She is the second oldest of 7 siblings. Writing has been a passion of her from a very young age. Through writing, Priscilla has been able to express her intricate thoughts and emotions. Since her childhood, she has dreamed of writing her own books, and now that dream has come to fruition. Besides writing, she enjoys music, sports, and going to the gym.

www.ingramcontent.com/pod-product-compliance
Lightning Source LLC
LaVergne TN
LVHW092055060526
838201LV00047B/1394